D1112609

The Vegetable Patch

THE VEGETABLE PATCH

Copyright © Summersdale Publishers Ltd, 2013

Illustrations by Debbie Powell
With text by Anna Martin

Summersdale Publishers Ltd
46 West Street
Chichester
West Sussex
PO19 1RP
UK

www.summersdale.com

Printed and bound in the Czech Republic

ISBN: 978-1-84953-377-5

Substantial discounts on bulk quantities of Summersdale books are available to corporations, professional associations and other organisations. For details contact Nicky Douglas by telephone: +44 (0) 1243 756902, fax: +44 (0) 1243 786300 or email: nicky@summersdale.com.

The Vegetable Patch

Tips and Advice for
Growing Your Own

Isobel Carlson

summersdale

Introduction

There's nothing more satisfying than growing and harvesting your own delicious produce, but starting and maintaining a kitchen garden can be daunting. Knowing what, when and where to plant and dealing with unforeseen problems, such as pests and diseases, is enough to test the most competent gardener. That's where this handy little book comes in, providing bite-size tips and gentle prompts of tasks to be done in the edible garden, season by season. Keep it in your pocket and jot down your own notes and observations to get the best out of your vegetable patch year after year.

Before You Start

Before venturing out into the garden, write a list of your household's favourite vegetables and herbs. Go through your cookery books containing seasonal recipes and plan your vegetable planting around much-loved dishes. Don't grow too much of any one thing but enough of the crops that you love.

The absolute essentials that no gardener should be without are: a trusty spade, trowel, rake, hoe, fork, wheelbarrow, secateurs, shears, lawnmower (not for the courtyard gardener), and protective gardening gloves. Make sure the larger tools are the right weight for you. Other items to keep handy include: plant labels, garden canes, a ball of string or twine (or even old bread ties or decommissioned tights or stockings) to secure plants with, and a clean-bladed pocketknife to cut off diseased leaves.

Although non-essential, a kneeler can take the ache out of gardening. You can buy kneelers, but you could just as easily make your own. Fill an old hot-water bottle with polystyrene chips for a waterproof and wipe-clean knee cushion to make those long gardening jobs a little more comfortable.

Draw a plan of your garden showing the path of the sun throughout the day. Be aware that many vegetable plants, such as peppers and tomatoes, need at least six hours of sunshine each day to thrive throughout those important growing and harvesting months. Other vegetable plants, such as spinach, salad leaves, beetroot and radishes, prefer cooler conditions and shade.

If you are a novice vegetable grower, try half a dozen crops in the first year and see how you get on. Good crops for beginners are beetroot, spinach, lettuce, courgettes, potatoes, runner beans and onions. Herbs are particularly low maintenance and many varieties will take care of themselves.

Key to a successful yield is crop rotation and, no matter how small your vegetable patch, you

should endeavour to follow the simple rule of
not growing the same crop in the same space two
years running. If you fail to rotate your planting
you will get a build-up of diseases specific to
the crop in question. On this note it's worth
remembering that potatoes and tomatoes both
come from the nightshade family and, therefore,
should not be planted consecutively in
the same spot.

Notes

....
....
....
....
....
....
....
....
....
....
....
....
....
....
....
....
....

Before You Start

....

....

....

....

....

....

....

....

....

....

....

....

....

....

....

....

....

....

Early Spring

ONE OF THE first jobs to do in spring is to prepare your beds for sowing. The soil needs to be 'tilthy' or 'friable', which is when it has the texture of breadcrumbs, i.e. fine and crumbly. Not many gardens are going to have the perfect loam, but they can be improved. Remember, it's important not to work saturated soil. Instead, wait for a spell of fine weather and, once the soil is drier and more workable, break down any clods with a fork and remove stones, then rake the soil twice, the first time to remove further stones and weeds and to thin the soil. The final sweep should leave your soil resembling fine breadcrumbs, which is the ideal consistency for planting.

IF YOU HAVE some old, failed guttering, don't throw it away as it can be adapted for irrigating the vegetable patch. Drill several small holes along the guttering and lay it alongside your row of vegetables. Water poured into the levelled

gutter will gradually drip through to the bases of your plants without disturbing the soil around their delicate roots. Similar irrigation devices can be made using old plastic milk containers. Simply pierce holes in the sides and around the bases and partially bury them in the vegetable patch. Fill them as required, and your fruit and vegetable crops will have a steady and gradual supply of water.

To CLEAR PREVIOUSLY uncultivated land of perennial weeds, cut them down, then cover the area with old carpet, thick cardboard or heavy-duty black polythene – cut up black bin liners, for example. Weigh the covering down with bricks to prevent it being blown off. Total exclusion of light will kill most weeds within a season. The more persistent varieties such as dandelions can take up to a year to die out completely.

As THE WEATHER begins to improve and the soil warms up, it's time to sow salad vegetables such as varieties of lettuce, rocket, beetroot, radish and onion. There is no need to germinate the seeds in a propagator at this time of year – plant directly into well-prepared soil containing garden compost. It's important that the soil is moist before you sow your seeds, so water it if necessary. If you haven't grown salad vegetables before, rocket is a great one for starting out as the slugs hate it!

ASIDE FROM SEED trays and seedling pots, there are all manner of things that can be employed to plant your seeds in, such as old newspapers rolled and fashioned into napkin-ring-shaped rounds, or finished toilet roll tubes cut into halves. Fill whatever receptacle you decide to use for planting with compost, add seeds according to planting instructions on the packet and water regularly. Once seedlings are ready to be planted out, take the round and transplant directly into the ground. The paper or cardboard will biodegrade and the root system of your seedling will not be destroyed.

ANOTHER CHEAP ALTERNATIVE to purchasing seed trays or seedling pots is to save packaging from shop-bought food items, such as cardboard egg boxes and drinks cartons, as these can be used as alternative planters. Supermarkets and greengrocers regularly throw away wooden and plastic crates, which make excellent trays to house pots.

IF YOU ARE reusing seedling pots from the previous season, it's best to sterilise them first just in case they are harbouring soil-borne fungus, insects or disease. Brush out any old debris then scrub the pots, and any drainage crocks, with water mixed with some detergent. Rinse and then dunk briefly in a dilute solution of water and disinfectant. Leave to dry in a well-ventilated place, remembering to turn the pots over so that both insides and outsides are dry. Then store in a cool, dry place, sorting the pots according to size.

CARROTS ARE A joy to grow but they can be susceptible to carrot fly. As a deterrent try planting onions near your crop as the smell can ward off these unwanted pests. Radishes can produce a similar effect if planted near to carrots, and they also repel maggots. Be sure to thin carrot seedlings and harvest full-grown roots during the evenings so as not to attract the carrot fly as they are less bothersome at this time of day ('thinning' involves the removal of excess plants in order to ensure that the ones remaining get the air, space and light they need to produce a healthy crop).

THE MOST TRADITIONAL method of sowing seeds is in neat rows along the length of the bed. To do this, mark out the rows with a piece of string (tie each end to bamboo canes that can be anchored in the soil to make the string taut). Using the tip of a trowel or the stick of a broom follow the line of the string to make a drill – a tiny trench – to the depth that you need to sow your seeds. Refer to the packet instructions on how deep and how closely to sow your seeds.

IDEALLY, YOU WANT your vegetable rows to run north to south, since the sun moves from

east to west, thus providing the plants with maximum sunlight.

ONE BASIC RULE of thumb when it comes to planting vegetable seed is: the larger the vegetable seed, the deeper it should be sown. Roughly speaking, smaller seeds such as onions, lettuces and carrots should be sown about 1.5 centimetres deep, whereas larger seeds such as cabbages should be about 2.5 centimetres deep and bean seeds 5 centimetres deep.

TO MAXIMISE YOUR vegetable plot, plant two vegetable crops in the same trench by mixing a fast-growing vegetable, such as lettuce, with a slow-growing one, such as parsnip or carrot. Alternatively, you can keep sowing the same type of vegetable every few weeks, waiting for the previous crop to be at the thinning stage before sowing again. Lettuce and radish are ideal for this, enabling you to 'cut and come again' throughout the summer months.

PLANT OUT ARTICHOKE suckers in spring. Suckers are the underground runners or side shoots that form at the bases of plants, shrubs and trees. These can grow to over a metre in height and width and this needs to be considered when deciding where to plant them. Choose a sunny spot with well-drained soil and add plenty of well-rotted manure. Each plant can produce around a dozen edible heads. Do not allow plants to become dry so water regularly (every few days) until the plants are established. The artichokes can be harvested in the second year. In the first year, you will need to remove flower heads as they appear.

AUBERGINES NEED TO be sown early, around February/March. It's best to grow them inside in pots containing moist compost on a sunny windowsill at this time of year, but if you have a particularly sheltered spot and live in a milder climate then they can be planted outside. Allow bees to pollinate the plants when they come into flower by placing the pots outside on warm spring days.

BEETROOT CAN BE sown from mid-spring on a monthly basis until midsummer. Encourage the seeds to germinate by soaking them in water for a few hours before sowing in small batches in drills, at a depth of about 2.5 centimetres and allowing 5 centimetres between each cluster. After sowing, rake the soil back over the drill. Beetroot tends to germinate within two to three weeks, at which time you can thin out the clusters to 7.5 centimetres apart. The thinned plants can be eaten as a salad crop.

ONCE YOU'VE SOWN your crops, plant a few French marigolds as these will repel pests, protecting your precious vegetables.

DEADHEAD FLOWERS (i.e. pull off the spent flower heads) on rhubarb as soon as they appear in the spring, as allowing the flowers to set seed will weaken the plant and thus reduce the harvest.

ENSURE A BUMPER apple harvest in autumn by scattering cooled bonfire ashes around the bases

of your fruit trees in the spring. The ash must
be from a wood fire. Loganberries, raspberries,
blueberries and strawberries will also benefit from
some of this cheap 'potash'.

SCRAPE AWAY THE topsoil around the roots of
gooseberry bushes to expose any soil in which
the gooseberry sawfly has laid its eggs – the
larvae of which will demolish the tender plants
if given the opportunity. Birds will feast on the
eggs and larvae and save you from needing to use
pesticides.

As SOON AS the weather begins to warm up, it's
time to plant out your chitted early potatoes.
'Chitting' means germinating the potatoes before
planting (see page 118 on when and how to start
the chitting process). Dig a trench around 10
centimetres deep and add a little fertiliser before
planting. Handle the tubers very carefully so
as not to break any of the delicate shoots, and
place the tubers in the trench with their shoots
pointing upwards. Cover the tubers with soil.
Be on the lookout for shoots breaking the soil's

surface and keep covering with soil – you should find that each plant has a little mound of earth around it. The potato tubers will need some basic frost protection, such as horticultural fleece or cloches, but if you don't have these, an effective and cheaper alternative is to use sheets of newspaper weighted down with stones. It might look unattractive but you can remove the coverings in the daytime.

ANOTHER CHEAP ALTERNATIVE
to the glass cloche is to make your own from used plastic drinks bottles. Cut the bottoms off and stand them upright, firmly embedded in the ground, to protect the plants from slugs. Remove the bottle tops only when the plants are more established, to allow them to acclimatise.

PURCHASE ONION SETS for planting now, or plant the bulbs that you have grown yourself from seed. Onion sets are small, immature onions. Find a well-drained plot that receives plenty of sunshine and plant them out in shallow drills. Cover the bulbs so that the necks are protruding slightly above the soil.

GARLIC CAN BE planted out now, see pages 98 and 118 for growing advice.

PLANT OUT BARE-ROOTED soft fruit trees now, such as nectarine, apricot and peach. Choose a sheltered spot that receives plenty of sunlight. See page 105 for advice on planting bare-rooted trees. A south-facing wall or fence is ideal. As these trees tend to blossom in early spring, when few insects are about, it's a good idea to help with the pollination. Gently brush the pollen between the flowers, preferably on a sunny day. These tender plants will also require frost protection. Wrap the trunks with horticultural fleece, which will also go some way to prevent the spread of Peach Leaf Curl (a fungal disease that causes disorted leaves).

PLANT SUMMER CABBAGES and carrots under cloches or peg out some polythene to keep the

worst of the frost away. Outsmart the white cabbage moth by laying a few whole sheets of scrunched-up kitchen towel around cabbages and broccoli. This will lead the moth to believe that the territory is already patrolled by other moths and it won't lay eggs there. To eradicate mildew that may appear on leaves as your cabbage plants mature, pick off and destroy the affected leaves and treat the plants with a fungicide.

CLUBROOT IS A FUNGAL growth particularly common in Brassicas (e.g. cabbage and broccoli), but a handy tip to employ when planting your greens out is to drop a cube of rhubarb directly into each planting hole before putting the plant on top. It may seem an odd suggestion but the rhubarb releases oxalic acid, which prevents clubroot from attacking the roots of the Brassica plants.

ONCE THE AIR temperature is over 15 degrees Celsius, you can consider growing citrus plants in pots outdoors. As there is still a risk of frost at this time of year, it's important to keep an eye on the weather forecast as citrus plants can die in freezing conditions. Garden centres tend to sell citrus as mature potted plants but you can try growing from seeds from fresh fruit at any time of year if the plants are to remain indoors. Spring is the best time to repot any citrus plants that you already have. Only use the next size pot and treat the plants to some specially formulated citrus compost, which is available from garden centres.

SOW EARLY CARROTS in early spring but give them a bit of protection from the cold temperatures with some cloches. Treat your carrot seeds to fresh manure mixed with some old coffee grounds so that they grow straight and tall.

PREPARE THE GROUND for planting peas at the onset of milder weather. The soil needs to be warm and not too wet, so begin by covering the designated area with polythene. Create a drill roughly 5 centimetres deep and 30 centimetres wide, then water well before planting the seeds 5 centimetres apart, in three rows. If you want a succession of peas, plant seeds every fortnight.

NOW THAT THE weather is a little milder, it's time to begin sowing lettuce, leeks, asparagus, broad beans, spinach, endive and salad leaves. Seeds can be sown outside, but keep an eye on the weather forecast for frost and have some horticultural fleece or cloches at the ready. Butterflies are repelled by the smell of tomato plants, so plant these amongst your leeks to prevent them laying eggs on your crop.

PLANT OUT STRAWBERRY plants from late March. It's a good idea to plant new ones every two to three years as yields diminish dramatically after the first few years and they become more prone to pests and diseases. Position your strawberry patch in a sunny spot and preferably out of the wind. Place the strawberry plants roughly 35 centimetres apart and in rows that are 70 centimetres apart and water well. Place straw under the fruits once they begin to form, to avoid them coming into contact with the soil. The straw layer also helps to suppress weeds. Barley straw is the best type to use for this, as it's soft and pliable.

STRAWBERRIES ALSO GROW well in hanging baskets. This is also a very effective way of ensuring the fruits don't succumb to slugs. Plant half a dozen plants in a basket and water every day. Give them a boost once a fortnight with some plant food such as tomato feed. See page 56 for information on harvesting strawberries.

MAKE A THOROUGH check of any fruit or vegetables that have been stored away over winter. Be on the lookout for signs of rodent activity as well as any produce that has rotted. Throw any past-their-best fruit and vegetables onto the compost heap.

OPEN YOUR GREENHOUSE doors and vents on warm days to allow the air to circulate. If you are starting off your seedlings in a greenhouse, you can reduce your heating costs on cooler days by hanging plastic sheeting across the greenhouse and only heating the area that

contains the seedlings. Use bubble wrap to insulate the door and block any draughts.

Herb plants become readily available in garden centres at this time of year so consider planting up a few. Different herbs prefer different conditions; for example, rosemary, thyme, chives and oregano prefer full sun, which makes them ideal for growing in a window box or on the kitchen windowsill, whereas parsley, chervil and wild rocket prefer some shade. Both sun-loving and shade-loving herbs thrive in moist soil-based compost.

Train the new growth on grapevines by constructing a support system with lengths of horizontal wire threaded through 'vine eyes' attached to a wall or inside the greenhouse, depending on whether they are being grown inside or outdoors.

Start off Brussels sprouts in the greenhouse now. These plants are particularly slow-growing, taking around thirty weeks to crop, but they can be harvested throughout winter, so you'll have fresh, home-produced sprouts for Christmas dinner!

KEEP AN EYE out for weed growth throughout the spring, as the younger the weed the easier it will be to pull it up. Be sure to dig up the roots to prevent regrowth – a hoe is great for this task.

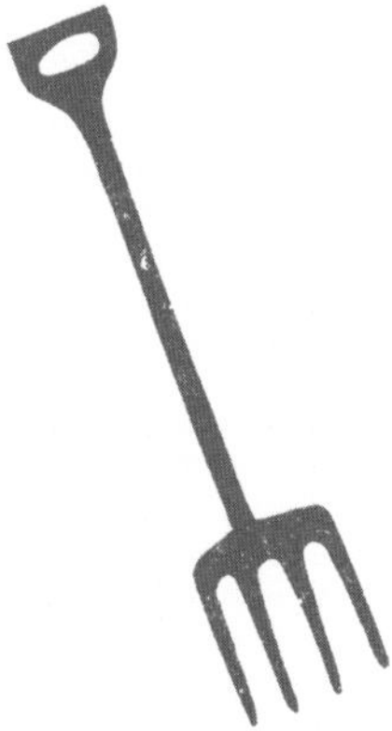

Notes

....

....

....

....

....

....

....

....

....

....

....

....

....

....

....

....

....

....

Early Spring

....

....

....

....

....

....

....

....

....

....

....

....

....

....

....

....

....

....

Late Spring

CHECK YOUR APPLES for apple scab during late spring. This is an airborne fungus that survives through the winter months on leaves, so it's important to collect up and bin or burn foliage that appears infected. The fungus appears as olive-green blotches on leaves and black blotches on fruit, and it can cause blistering on new shoots. Cut away and dispose of any infected shoots, fruits and leaves, and check your apple trees every couple of weeks for signs of scab until after the autumn harvest.

HANG BEE-FRIENDLY wasp traps on fruit trees and vines by stringing up jam jars containing a mixture of vinegar, sugar and salt. Wasps are attracted to sweet and sour flavours whereas bees steer clear of the sour mixture.

WHEN THE FRUIT trees and bushes have finished blossoming, apply a mulch round the bases of

the plants as this gives them all the nutrients they need to produce a healthy and abundant crop. It also reduces the amount of weed growth and conserves moisture around the roots in the summer months.

CONTINUE TO PROTECT strawberries at night from late frosts with a double-layer covering of horticultural fleece or cloches, but make sure that these are removed during the day to allow access to bees for pollination. Replenish straw around the plants so that the fruits don't touch the soil and air circulates well around the plant. Keep an eye out for grey mould, which is a common disease of soft fruit. A fuzzy grey mould will be evident on leaves, buds and fruit. To reduce the risk of grey mould, regularly remove dead and dying leaves and thin out plants so that they are well ventilated.

FRUIT TREES AND bushes may also need further overnight frost protection. Smaller trees and bushes can be covered with horticultural fleece.

Fruit growing on fences and walls can be draped with fleece or hessian, making sure that the fabric doesn't touch the blossoms.

CUT UP AN old pair of tights and use the pieces to tie up soft fruit and other crops to supports. The stretchiness of the material will allow the plant to grow without becoming damaged or restricted.

KEEP UP WITH the weeding and watering of fruit trees and bushes. Regularly hoe around the bases of these plants and trim away any suckers that have formed. New trees will be particularly vulnerable to drought so keep the bases well watered.

START HARVESTING RHUBARB from late spring right through to the autumn. Wait until the leaves are fully open before pulling. The colour of the rhubarb is also a good indicator of its readiness for harvesting – it should be dark pink. Gently

twist the stems and pull from the base of the plant.

CONTINUE WITH SUCCESSIONAL sowing of peas, salad leaves and broad beans. Sowing small amounts at fortnightly intervals will ensure a plentiful supply throughout the summer months. Sow them into a prepared bed of soil thoroughly mixed with manure or compost.

PLANTS THAT HAVE been seeded directly into the soil will need to be thinned out now to avoid overcrowding. This is particularly the case with root vegetables. Thinning the plants will encourage higher yields. The plants will also be healthier as they won't be fighting for nutrients and the air will be able to circulate, reducing the risk of disease. Seedlings will need to be thinned when they are around 5 to 10 centimetres in height and with at least a couple of sets of leaves. Do your thinning when the ground is damp as it will be easier to pull up and dislodge plants more cleanly and without disturbing neighbouring roots. It's also a good idea to do this job in the evening so that the remaining plants have time to adjust before feeling the heat of full sun. Thinning salad crops tends to be straightforward as they have shallower roots, but root vegetables, such as carrots, beetroots and onions, can be more difficult as disturbing the roots when they're young can cause the vegetables to split or deform. Therefore, you should trim root-vegetable seedlings at soil level rather than pulling them. Refer to the instructions on the seed packet for advice on how much space individual plants require for healthy growth.

PROTECT YOUR BURGEONING fruit plants from birds by stringing up a home-made bird-scarer made from unwanted shiny objects, such as old cutlery (spoons are best for safety reasons!), CDs and foil cases, strung together with twine. A home-made fruit cage is also a good idea; see page 114 for information on how to make one. There are many different methods that gardeners use to scare birds. Another idea to try is to balance small yoghurt pots and washing balls upside down on canes planted in the garden. When the wind catches them, the rattling noise

should scare the birds away. The pots also save you from impaling yourself on the sharp ends of the canes! You could also try to cut up a past-repair garden hose into small pieces as these short lengths of tube resemble snakes. Paint patterns on them and distribute round the vegetable patch to frighten away rodents, birds and cats.

THOUGH THE WEATHER is just beginning to warm up, it's time to look ahead to Halloween and plant pumpkin seeds in containers filled with compost. Make sure the seeds are planted on their sides, one seed per pot and at a depth of around 3 centimetres. Give them a good water and place the pots on windowsills to germinate. Once the roots begin to show, repot the seedlings in a slightly larger pot. Then, once the plants are more established, prepare an area of garden by forking in well-rotted manure or compost before planting approximately 2.5 metres apart. Alternatively, seeds can be sown directly into the ground from late May in a sunny, sheltered spot.

KEEP AN EYE on your pea plants, because once they have grown to around 8 centimetres in height they will need supports to continue growing up. Plant canes or use netting, or for a more decorative option, use branches or strong twigs. Drive them into the ground at roughly half-metre intervals for your pea plants to climb. Old curtain rods, particularly extendable ones, also make excellent supports for climbing plants. Simply extend the rod as the plant grows.

SLUGS ARE THE bane of every gardener's life and there are many methods employed in the removal of them. Slugs can't abide copper, as it gives them an electric shock on contact, which means that copper bands placed on trees, containers and raised beds can be very useful in repelling the critters. The bands need to be wide enough so that slugs can't raise their bodies up and over them – as many shop-bought copper bands aren't wide enough to stop the slugs it's best to fix two side by side for a greater width. A much cheaper and equally effective solution for pot-grown plants is to apply

Vaseline around the rims of the pots to stop the slimy pests in their tracks. Slugs and earwigs are both partial to beer, so simply fill a few shallow dishes with beer and watch the slugs and earwigs congregate.

MAKE GARLIC WATER to spray on your new plants as this will also deter slugs. This can be prepared by crushing a couple of garlic cloves into a litre of water and bringing the liquid to the boil in a saucepan. Leave the liquid to cool then strain it before pouring into a bottle with an airtight lid. When watering your seedlings, add a tablespoon of the garlic water for every 4–5 litres of water in your watering can. Make sure to repeat this after wet weather so that the plants remain protected.

PINCH OUT THE tops of aubergine plants when they are roughly 40 centimetres in height. This encourages fruit to grow on the side shoots rather than the main stem. Feed with a standard fertiliser until the fruits are formed, then use a tomato feed every one to two weeks.

Late Spring

FROST IS STILL prevalent at this time of year so keep a regular eye on the weather forecast and have plenty of horticultural fleece or polythene handy to cover your plants at night. Remember to pin this down with stakes if wind is expected, taking care not to damage delicate plants.

START THINNING OUT grapevines now. This will reduce the stress on the vines and the remaining grapes will be healthier and tastier. Use narrow scissors for this delicate job, which requires snipping off individual berries so that the air can circulate round the remaining ones, reducing the risk of fungal problems. Remove at least a quarter of the berries and any tendrils. Tie the leader and lateral vines to supports with string, twine or pieces of fabric cut from old pairs of tights.

PLANT OUT YOUR greenhouse-grown seedlings now, such as runner and French beans, cucumbers, courgettes and marrows. Refer to the packet instructions as to how much space the plants require and for growing conditions.

FORCED RHUBARB TASTES particularly good. Once the rhubarb harvest has finished for the year, dig up some roots – three-year-old ones are best. Leave plenty of soil on the roots and repot into large containers. These pots must remain outside for a few nights of frost to help the buds to grow. Once thoroughly chilled, move the pots indoors to a warm, dark spot, such as a cellar or cupboard.

Alternatively the rhubarb can be forced outside in a plastic dustbin insulated with straw or horse manure. Cover the rhubarb roots with more soil, leaving only the growing bud exposed. Keep moist. Start to harvest the stalks when they are around 30 centimetres high. This should take around twelve weeks. The harvesting period lasts about a month and then the roots can go outside once again, but place mulch over them for protection over the winter and allow them to rest for a year. It's a good idea to have more than one crown so that you can force the crowns in alternate years.

APPLE TREES AND other hardy fruit trees
need pruning in late spring to maintain fruit
production and the health of the plant. Wait
for a fine day, then carefully inspect the tree,
first for dead limbs, which should be easy to
spot as the blossom will be out at this time and
these branches will not have any blooms. Next,
prune away any diseased branches, or ones that
are growing upwards or downwards instead
of straight out. Trim away a few inches of new
growth to allow the air to get to the mature
blooms. To prune the branches you will need a
hacksaw or pruning blade and some cloth tape.
Mark out where the cuts need to be made using
the cloth tape. Make sure the cutting point is
past the branch collar, as cutting beyond this will
weaken the tree. The collar is a wrinkly looking
section of bark near the base of the tree limb.
Begin by trimming the top branches first and
gradually work your way down the
tree. Finish off by pruning away any
suckers that are growing at the
base of the tree. Suckers are
seedlings that will grow into
new trees if left and will drain
the nutrients from the existing

tree. Once the pruning is done, give the tree an
extra helping hand by digging in some manure
round the base.

PRUNE BACK AUTUMN-FRUITING raspberry canes
to around 10 centimetres. Retain the cut canes
because they can be used as supports for your peas.

CONSIDER WAYS TO collect and store rainwater
for the warm, dry months ahead. A water butt
can collect water from the roof of a house,
garage, or any structure that has gutters and a
drainpipe. Grey water, which is domestic waste
water, such as bath water and washing-up water,
can also be used to water plants, but it's best not
to use grey water on salad plants and other fruits
and vegetables that do not require cooking. It's
important never to store grey water as harmful
organisms can develop; use it as and when it
becomes available.

SOW MAINCROP VARIETIES of carrots now. They
should not need any frost protection at this time.

CABBAGE ROOT FLY can make an unwelcome appearance at this time of year. It stunts the growth of plants and the maggots of the fly eat their way through the roots, eventually killing the plants. Plants most commonly affected include Brassicas, turnips, radishes and swedes. The only way to remove them is by digging up all of the infected plants, which must then be binned or burned. Brassicas must not be planted for three years in the infected plot. Prevention is better than cure, however, and one of the most effective ways of avoiding an infestation is to place a collar of old carpet or thick cardboard around each plant. This prevents the cabbage root fly from laying its eggs in close proximity to the plants.

WHEN YOUR COURGETTES have come into flower, you can pick the flowers and make delicious stuffed fritters using the following recipe:

Stuffed Courgette Fritters

Tear up six courgette flowers into pieces. Make
a simple pancake batter by mixing 50 grams of
self-raising flour and an egg, a pinch of salt and
pepper and a little water. Add the flower pieces
to the batter, then heat some oil in a frying pan.
When the pan is hot, pour a dollop of the batter
and flower mixture into the pan and fry until
golden brown on both sides. Serve immediately.
For a slightly more substantial meal, add in
some thinly sliced courgette to the
batter mixture.

Notes

....
....
....
....
....
....
....
....
....
....
....
....
....
....
....
....
....
....

Late Spring

Early Summer

REGULARLY WATER CITRUS plants and spray the leaves with a fine mist in the early mornings. Use a summer feed on citrus plants to encourage a good crop and to keep the plant strong. The plants can remain outside throughout the summer, but place them in a sheltered spot to protect them from cooler winds.

KEEP A CLOSE eye on container plants on warm summer days as they will need to be watered every day. Keep a full watering can close by so that you can top them up in the early mornings, and in the evenings too if necessary.

CUCUMBER SEEDS CAN be sown outside now, provided they are placed in a sunny, sheltered spot. To help the seeds germinate before planting, place them on a piece of damp kitchen towel for a couple of days until the root starts to emerge

from the seed coat. Plant the seeds around half
a centimetre apart into compost or well-rotted
manure. Once your seedling emerges and you
can count a minimum of six leaves on the main
and side shoots, use your thumb and
forefinger to pinch out the new growth
of the plant. Water well and feed
with a liquid fertiliser as soon
as the fruits start to develop.

HARVEST WALNUTS IN early
summer when the nuts are still
green, otherwise the squirrels will do their best
to pinch the lot. Store them by pickling them in
fortified wine or vinegar in an airtight jar. Wait
until they have turned black before eating them
– this colour change takes about five days. They
will keep for around eighteen months and taste
particularly good with cold meats.

THE FIRST CROP of beetroot will be ready for
harvesting now – at around eight weeks after
they were sown. Harvest every other plant in the
row to allow the rest of the plants to develop

further. Gently pull the beetroots from the soil.
They should be about 2.5 centimetres in diameter.
Store them by placing a layer of sand about 5
centimetres deep at the bottom of a container
and laying the beetroots on the sand, making sure
they are not touching, then cover them with sand
and repeat the process until the container is full.
The same storage method can be used for carrots
and potatoes. The container can be
anything from an old crate to
a chest of drawers, and it
must be kept in cool, dry
conditions.

PLANT BRUSSELS SPROUTS outside now. They prefer
a sheltered spot and plenty of space to spread out –
allow at least 75 centimetres between plants.

EARLY CARROTS WILL also be ready for harvesting in
early summer. Carrot fly could become a problem at
this time of year and these nasty pests can destroy
an entire crop by tunnelling into the roots of carrots
and other edible crops. The carrot fly can only fly
to about 60 centimetres, so it's worth considering

planting maincrop carrots in raised beds or high-sided containers, such as old tyres (see pages 53–55 for more information on container planting). Covering the plants with horticultural fleece will also go some way to protecting the crop. Once the carrot fly has taken hold, however, it's necessary to introduce pesticides.

KEEP AN EYE on your potato crop for emerging foliage and cover with soil as soon as it appears. Early potatoes may be ready for harvesting now. Choose a dry day to check the progress of underground growth. Carefully dig away the soil with a trowel around one plant to check for size. Cut the above-ground growth off a fortnight before lifting the crop as this will help toughen the skins of the potatoes, making them less likely to become damaged when lifted and stored.

CHECK ON YOUR greenhouse-grown tomatoes and simulate pollination simply by tapping the flowers with your finger.

It is essential to keep watering your crops, especially if there are prolonged periods of warm, dry weather. Make sure to invest in a water butt that is connected to a downpipe from a gutter (see page 43 for information on water butts). Rainwater can be preserved in this way and beats using a hosepipe to water plants in the summer.

Check the grease bands around fruit trees and replace where necessary (see page 105 for information on grease bands). Some species of moth, namely those with wingless females that climb the trunks to lay their eggs, are still active in April.

Don't be alarmed if your fruit trees start to lose a lot of fruit at this time. This phenomenon is known as 'June drop' and it's nature's way of thinning out the crop so that the strongest and healthiest fruits remain.

Sow more salad leaves now, as well as beetroot and radish. These make ideal container plants

if you are short on space. Containers come in
all shapes and sizes – be inventive by using an
old sink, toilet or even a wheelbarrow or coal
scuttle. The most important prerequisite when
it comes to choosing a receptacle for planting
is that it has drainage holes so that the roots of
plants don't become waterlogged, as this causes
them to rot. Salad vegetables with shallow roots,
such as lettuce, beetroot and radish, are ideal
for container planting as they only require a
depth of approximately 20 centimetres to thrive.
Root vegetables such as carrots and onions,
on the other hand, need a depth of around 50
centimetres, so it's important to bear this in
mind when choosing your containers. Keep them
regularly watered as they will dry out more
quickly than those planted in the vegetable patch.

ASK YOUR LOCAL garage for
old tyres to use as planters for
potatoes or carrots.
They're eco-friendly
and effective. For
carrots, a sandy soil
mix in a two-deep

tyre container will give you lovely, straight crops,
free of pests (remember, carrot fly can only fly to
around 60 centimetres so if the tyre wall is high
enough they cannot attack young plants). For
potatoes, plant chitted tubers one tyre deep, wait
for plants to grow, bank up with soil and add
more tyres to the stack (up to about three
tyres deep).

PLANTING SEEDS IN a container
is very different to planting in
the ground: all the nutrients
and water necessary for the plant
to grow must be contained within the pot, and
there's restricted room for root growth. Be sure
to consider this when choosing your pot and
the proposed contents. Make sure that the base
is off the ground – have bricks underneath, for
example, so that any excess water can drain out,
which will prevent roots from rotting.

EVEN IF YOUR garden extends to little more than
a narrow balcony, you can still successfully grow
fruit trees in containers – dwarf trees are ideally

suited to this and a sunny south-facing spot is best. Choose wood or plastic containers rather than terracotta pots, because while terracotta may look more attractive the plants inside them tend to dry out more quickly than those in plastic or wooden pots, and they are much heavier. A large pot is preferable – about 50-centimetres diameter – to ensure that the tree doesn't become pot-bound.

Choose from dwarf varieties of citrus trees, including lemons, limes and oranges, as well as dwarf versions of orchard fruits such as apples, pears and cherries. Container trees don't reach the height of those planted in the ground, but the fruit they produce will be of normal size and just as delicious.

IF YOU ARE 'potting on', a handy tip is to put the smaller pot inside the bigger one and fill around it with soil so that the space left when you lift the small pot out is the right size for the plant to go back into.

COURGETTES WILL NEED to be picked regularly at this time of year – as much as three times a week – to prevent them from becoming marrows and to ensure that the plants remain productive throughout the season.

PLACE NETTING OVER the strawberry patch to help protect the ripening fruits from the clutches of squirrels and birds. The fruit should be ready to pick from July onwards. It's important to pick the strawberries as soon as they are ripe as they don't keep for long. Keep the stalks attached to the strawberries when harvesting as it helps to maintain their freshness.

IF YOU HAVE a glut of soft fruits, you can 'open-freeze' them as soon as they have been picked by laying them on trays and placing them in the freezer. Once completely frozen, 'decant' them into plastic bags and seal them. Alternatively, make jam using a recipe such as this one:

Fruit Jam

To make a basic fruit jam, first warm 850 grams of caster sugar on a baking tray in a preheated oven at 120 degrees Celsius for about ten minutes. Crush 500 grams of hulled strawberries in a large bowl with a potato masher. When the sugar is warm and runny, stir it in with the strawberries and leave for four hours at room temperature, stirring occasionally. Mix in one sachet of pectin crystals or half a bottle of the liquid form, along with three tablespoons of lemon juice. Ladle the mixture into sterilised jars, cover and leave to set at room temperature for around three hours. If it has difficulty setting by this point, add another tablespoon of lemon juice. The jam should be fully set and ready to eat in 24 hours. Enjoy with home-made scones.

BEGIN HARVESTING PEAS now. It's important to keep on top of this to secure the freshest peas. Start from the bottom of the plant and work your way up. Save seeds for next year by leaving a few seed pods to dry out on the plant – peas are one of the easiest seeds for the novice seed-saver. Wait until the pods are bone dry before picking them, then remove the seeds from the pods. Then store in a labelled envelope or lidded container until it's time to plant them.

GIVE YOUR VEGETABLE crops a helping hand by feeding them regularly with a liquid feed to increase their yield. Tomatoes, aubergines and peppers in particular benefit from the administration of liquid tomato feed. If you're growing these crops in the greenhouse, it's a good idea to check for red spider mites at this time of year. These pests can be washed off the plants as often as necessary with plenty of soapy water.

WATER POTTED HERBS in the early mornings, especially on warm days. In addition, use a feed once a week in the summer months to boost leaf production. To help potted herbs grow better keep the soil fertilised with banana skins as these are a good source of potassium. Cut up pieces of banana peel and add directly to the soil.

IT MIGHT BE getting a little hot in the greenhouse now and it may not be enough to keep the door

and air vents open on warm days, so to provide some protection for your indoor crops, as they could become scorched, consider investing in some blinds or applying shading paint to the glass.

KEEP ON TOP of the weeds over the early summer, because just as crops are starting to thrive so will the weeds. It's far easier to pull up weeds when they are less established as they are less likely to disturb neighbouring plants. Always do your weeding in dry conditions and before the weeds have had the chance to come into flower. If you do your weeding in damp conditions, you will end up dividing and spreading the weeds over a larger area.

LOOK OUT FOR brown rot infection on apples, pears, cherries, plums and other fruit from midsummer. This fungal disease turns fruit brown with small off-white pustules. It's important to remove rotten fruit from the tree to reduce the spread of the infection.

Notes

....
....
....
....
....
....
....
....
....
....
....
....
....
....
....
....

Early Summer

....
....
....
....
....
....
....
....
....
....
....
....
....
....
....
....
....
....
....

Late Summer

PINCH OUT RUNNER bean tips that have reached the top of their supports, as this forces the plant to grow side shoots, which increases crop yield as well as keeping it tidy. In addition, pinch out side shoots on tomatoes, so that the plant's energy is concentrated on producing the fruit rather than the side shoots. This is a task that must be undertaken regularly so that the main stems remain strong and healthy.

LATE SUMMER IS a peak time for composting, so make sure to regularly top up your compost heap with kitchen and garden waste. Aim for a quarter to half the compost to be made up of soft green materials (i.e. kitchen vegetable waste, grass cuttings and annual weeds) to feed the microorganisms. The rest of the heap should be made up of brown, woody waste, such as twigs, dead leaves, wood chippings, cardboard and paper. Layer soft green with dry brown matter

for best results. See pages 101–103 for more information on composting.

Now's the time to harvest shallots, onions and garlic. Wait for the leaves to turn yellow and wilt. Allow the bulbs to remain in the ground for up to a fortnight after the leaves have wilted so that they can mature fully. Pull up the bulbs, preferably on a sunny day, and leave them in the sunshine for a day to dry out. Then cure (dry out) the onions in a warm, dry place, away from sunlight, until the skins 'rattle' and the roots have become brittle and wiry. The onions can then be stored in net bags or in an old pair of tights, making sure to tie a knot between each onion, thereby allowing each one to be well ventilated – these can be hung up in the shed, pantry, or any cool, dry and shady spot. When you need to take an onion, simply cut below the knot.

Continue to sow salad crops throughout the summer and water regularly.

HAVE A CAREFUL look at your cucumbers now as the size, colour and firmness of the fruits will determine whether they are ready for picking. The skin should be a medium to dark green colour and the fruit should feel firm when squeezed. Cucumber sizes vary according to variety, so check on the seed packet for this information. Harvest regularly as this will encourage the vines to keep producing fruits.

REMOVE FOLIAGE AROUND pumpkins and squashes so that they can ripen in the sunshine. Raise the fruits onto bricks or straw beds for ventilation and to reduce the risk of slug damage.

PRUNE SOFT FRUIT trees, such as apricot, peach and nectarine, after they have fruited, and prune damson and plum trees straight after harvesting. See page 42 for general tree-pruning information.

KEEP WATERING CROPS – preferably with collected rainwater – on a regular basis, particularly those in containers, new plants or those growing against a wall, as irregular watering can cause splitting in root vegetable tubers and blossom end rot in tomato fruit.

KEEP LIFTING (HARVESTING) potatoes. Remember to compost the leaves unless they look faded or diseased, in which case consign them to the bin.

TIDY UP THE strawberry patch after the berries have fruited by removing old leaves and straw. This can be composted.

THE FRUITS OF an indoor melon crop will start to swell now. Allow the air to circulate round the fruits, reducing the risk of rot, by placing stone slabs under the fruit. For greenhouse-grown melons, supporting the weighty fruits using string bags or a strong pair of tights will keep the fruits off the ground and is an excellent way of reducing rot.

REMOVE SUCKERS SPROUTING from the bases of fruit trees by tearing them as this reduces regrowth. If left, they can quickly take root.

CHECK YOUR CROPS for aphids (e.g. greenfly or blackfly). Squash them between your finger and thumb, or use an insecticide where there is an infestation.

AUBERGINES ARE READY to be harvested now. Pick them when the skins are firm and shiny. Leave them too long and the skin will develop a dull appearance and the fruits will taste bitter.

LOOK OUT FOR blight fungus on tomato and potato crops grown outside. The fungus appears as greyish-black blotches on leaves and stems, and the fruits will become discoloured. Dispose of any infected plants by binning or burning them – never compost them.

LATE SUMMER IS a particularly busy time in the edible garden as many crops become ripe for harvesting, the other main ones being French and runner beans, tomatoes, courgettes, sweetcorn, soft fruits such as strawberries, grapes and raspberries, and early apples and pears.

HARVEST ARTICHOKE HEADS in the second year of growth. Pick the top bud first and then the side buds, before their scales have begun to open. Cut the buds with a few centimetres of stem still attached.

CONTINUE TO SOW vegetables, such as broad beans, dwarf beans, mung beans, beetroot, broccoli, cabbage, carrots, celeriac, endive, kale, lettuce and spring onions for this year, as well as next year's pak choi, peas, cauliflowers, chicory, coriander, radish and turnip.

SWEETCORN COBS WILL soon be ready to harvest, when the silky tassels on the top of the cobs have turned brown. Pull back a few of the leaves to check that the kernels are golden and press a kernel with your fingernail – if they are ripe and ready for picking, a creamy-coloured liquid will ooze from the kernel; if the liquid is watery it will need a little more time to ripen and if the liquid is thick and doughy, the corn is overripe.

YOU MIGHT FIND that you're rushed off your feet amid all the harvesting, but if you have a spare few moments, giving your greenhouse a bit of attention will pay dividends. Begin by cleaning as many surfaces as possible, as this will significantly reduce the incidence and spread of pests and diseases. Keep the greenhouse well ventilated on sunny days and reduce the risk of overheating by applying shading paint or erecting some blinds to provide shade for your ripening crops.

REGULARLY EXAMINE GREENHOUSE plants for whitefly. Rather than using chemicals to remove them – which is not recommended for edible

plants – make a trap for the pests by planting a sprinkle of flowering-tobacco seeds in a 10-centimetre-diameter pot filled with compost. When the plant has grown a few inches, hang the pot above any plants suffering from whitefly. Disturb the infested plants and the flies should decamp to the tobacco plant. When the tobacco plant is covered with flies, place a plastic bag over it and remove the plant, which can be composted once the flies are dead. Repeat the process if and when required and have a pre-prepared trap ready for damage limitation.

BEFORE GOING ON your summer holiday, enlist the help of a friend or neighbour to water your plants while you're away. Perhaps allow them to pick and keep some of your edible crops as a 'thank you'.

PINCH OUT THE tops of tomato plants to prevent them from growing too tall. This will also ensure that the growing fruits mature nicely.

Drying Herbs

Don't forget to harvest your herbs and dry out any excess for winter use. Sturdy herbs such as dill, bay, rosemary and oregano, can be air-dried on a windowsill. Moisture-rich herbs, such as basil, lemon balm and mint, are best oven-dried so that they dry out more quickly to avoid mould.

Before drying the herbs, cut and remove any dry or diseased leaves. Shake gently to remove any insects or rinse with cool water and pat dry with paper towels (wet herbs will mould and rot). Remove the lower leaves along the bottom inch or so of each branch. Bundle four to six branches together and tie as a bunch using string or a rubber band. The bundles will shrink as they dry and the rubber band will loosen, so check periodically that the bundle is not slipping.

Make small bundles of sturdy herbs for drying. Punch or cut several holes in a paper bag. Label the bag with the name of the herb to be dried and place the herb bundle upside down in the bag. Gather the ends of the bag around

the bundle and tie closed. Make sure the herbs are not crowded inside the bag. Hang the bag upside down in a warm, airy room and check in about two weeks to see how things are progressing. Keep checking weekly until the herbs are dry and ready to store.

Store your dried herbs in airtight containers in a cool, dark place. They should remain fresh for up to two years.

HARVEST SUMMER CABBAGES, kohlrabi and cauliflowers from July onwards. Cut the heads close to ground level with a sharp knife.

LOOK OUT FOR the flower shoots on green broccoli, making sure they are well formed, as this is the ideal time to harvest them. Once the flower buds have opened, the broccoli becomes tasteless.

Late Summer

Sow the following seeds in late summer: turnip, chicory, Chinese and spring cabbages, winter lettuce, broad beans and peas.

Summer-prune cordon and espalier apple and pear trees – these are trees that have been trained on wires or against trellises. Thin out the trees by removing damaged or weak fruits. Take your time over this and be careful to observe any signs of damage, such as moth larvae, which will appear as brown bumps on the fruits.

Some of the earlier-cropping apples and pears will be ready for harvesting now. Cup a ripe-looking fruit in your hand and give it a twist, if it's ripe it will come away easily, if not, it needs a little more time on the tree. Store harvested apples and pears by wrapping them individually in newspaper, but make sure they have no blemishes as they will rot quickly when stored. Use the damaged and bruised apples and pears for chutney, cider/perry, sauces and crumbles. If

you have room in your freezer, store fruit that is overripe until the winter months when it can be removed and defrosted to provide a treat for hungry birds in your garden.

HARVEST SUMMER-FRUITING raspberries now. This needs to be done regularly. The fruit is ripe when it's firm and can be plucked, leaving behind the plug that held it in place.

LOOK OUT FOR raspberry cane blight and raspberry spur blight in the summer months. Both of these infections can seriously damage the harvest and weaken the plant. Raspberry cane blight causes leaves to wither and the canes to become brittle, causing the bark to split and, in some cases, the canes to snap off easily. It's important to cut back the infected canes and to wipe the secateurs with disinfectant after each cut to prevent the infection from spreading. Raspberry spur blight is evident in the form of purple patches. Once again, the infected canes need to be cut and disposed of. Regular pruning and thinning of canes, along with mulching of the bases of the plant in spring (see page 32) and regular watering, will help reduce the risk of these diseases developing.

CONTINUE TO FEED tomato, pepper and aubergine plants regularly with a liquid high-potash feed. Try to reduce the amount of feed you mix into the water to a third of the recommended dose and apply it every time you water, rather than once a week with the recommended dose, for a bountiful crop.

ONCE YOUR PEA harvest is finished, cut the plants down to ground level and leave the roots to rot down as this releases nitrogen into the soil, which will boost the next crop.

PINCH OUT THE soft tips of the strongest branches on citrus plants. Look out for 'water shoots' (see page 119) and cut these back as they appear.

BE ON THE lookout for black vine weevil on container plants and soft fruit plants and trees.

It lays its eggs in the soil at the bases of plants and the larvae feeds off the plant's roots. These wingless, beetle-like bugs are very hard to spot but one of the telltale signs of vine weevil activity is when notches, or nibble marks, appear on leaves. The bugs are most active at night, so take a torch out into the garden and pick off the adult vine weevils as you see them. Do this nocturnal hunt once a week during the summer months – most of the adults will die once the cold weather sets in. Container plants that have been damaged or destroyed by vine weevil should be binned rather than composted in case the roots contain eggs or larvae. Protect your plants with netting as this goes some way to preventing the adult vine weevil from moving between plants.

MAKE A HERBAL vinegar salad dressing by using some of the herbs gathered from the garden (see pages 85–87) – rosemary, basil, parsley, fennel, coriander, for example:

Herbal Vinegar Salad Dressing

Tie the herbs together and leave to dry in a warm place. When the herbs are completely dry, find a tall clear glass bottle, sterilise it – with boiling water – and add the herbs. Fill the bottle with warmed white wine vinegar, making sure that the herbs are completely covered, as exposed herbs tend to go mouldy. Place the lid on the bottle and leave to infuse for a couple of months. If you are giving this as a present, you might like to sieve the mixture to remove the herbs and place some fresh stems in the bottle for decoration.

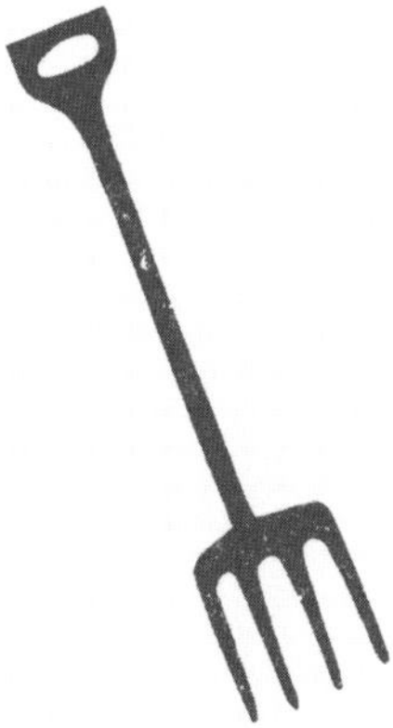

Notes

....
....
....
....
....
....
....
....
....
....
....
....
....
....
....
....
....

Late Summer

....
....
....
....
....
....
....
....
....
....
....
....
....
....
....
....
....
....

Early Autumn

CONTINUE TO PLANT new strawberry beds in early September. The soil will still be warm enough at this time for the plants to do a bit of growing before the dormant period. Give existing strawberry plants a good tidy-up by picking off and composting any discoloured leaves and harvested runners. It's important not to plant your strawberries near crops from the cabbage family (kohlrabi, kale, cauliflower, broccoli) as they do not make good bedfellows – the strawberry plants will cause the cabbage plants to deteriorate.

THE HARVESTING OF apples and pears begins in earnest in September. Look out for windfall fruit (fruit that has fallen from the tree) to determine which fruits are ready to pick.

GATHER UP WINDFALL and blemished fruit and make chutney using the following recipe:

Fruit Chutney

Cut away blemishes and remove the cores of a kilo of apples. Then remove the stones from a kilo of plums. Blend or finely chop the apples and plums with the same quantities of tomatoes and onions, before placing the mixture into a large saucepan with half a teaspoon each of cayenne pepper, mixed spice and mace and 500 grams of sultanas. Add 500 millilitres of vinegar and bring to the boil. When the fruit has softened, stir in 500 grams of sugar. Continue simmering the mixture for a couple of hours until it's nice and thick. Leave to cool, then decant the chutney into sterilised jars.

IF YOU HAVE a glut of apples, try making cider:

Home-made Cider

Choose a mixture of apple varieties, mixing
sweet (Morgan Sweet, for example) and sharp
(such as Crimson King). Use ripe ones from the
tree mixed with the windfall apples, leaving
them to stand for a few days to soften. You will
need a scratter (a device which mashes fruit)
to roughly pulp the apples. You will then need
an apple press. Pour some of the pulp over
a piece of muslin that's been laid within the
frame of the apple press. Fold the rest of the
muslin over the mixture and add another layer
of the mixture, and so on, until you have built
up enough layers to reach the top of the apple
press. Then begin to press the layers to extract
the apple juice, which collects in a container
below the press. Leave the juice to ferment for
several months in a covered container – add
yeast and sugar at your discretion; many cider
makers choose to let the juice ferment naturally.
While the juice is fermenting, you will need to
clear away the pips and stalks and any other

> apple debris from the liquid. When it is ready,
> decant the cider into sterilised bottles or a
> large keg, then drink!
>
> You can make perry, which is the pear version
> of cider, in the same way.

IT'S TIME TO dig up the remaining potatoes before
the slugs get to them. Carefully examine this final
crop for damage or infestation and leave on the
surface of the soil to dry out before storing in
hessian sacks in a cool, dark place, such as a shed
or garage.

HARVEST LATE-SOWN carrots and beetroots now.
If you have grown enough to store, choose only
the best ones and cut off their foliage
(see page 50 for storage advice).
Parsnips can remain in the ground
until after the first frost because
this makes them taste sweeter.

PUMPKINS WILL SOON be ripe for picking. It's important to do this before the first hard frost as this can destroy the fruits. Wait for the fruits to develop a deep uniform colour, then try pressing a thumbnail into the rind. If the rind resists denting, then it's ready to harvest. Handle the fruits very carefully to avoid bruising and splitting as these indentations can provide entrances for insects and rot-producing organisms. Keep pumpkins away from ripening fruit, as this will shorten the shelf life of the pumpkins.

CUT AWAY AND compost browning asparagus foliage. Watch out for spines as you go, and remove all debris around the crown to discourage asparagus beetle from making a home for itself over the winter. Prepare the bed for next year by adding grit to the soil.

IF YOUR TOMATOES don't appear to be ripening, either lay the fruits on a bed of straw and cover with a cloche or pull up the runners and hang them upside down in a shed or greenhouse.

Alternatively, use the green tomatoes to make chutney (see the chutney recipe on page 81).

CONTINUE TO PICK courgettes, cucumbers and runner, French and haricot beans to prolong the harvest until the first autumn frosts. Also harvest the last of the globe artichokes, gathering only the buds that are yet to open.

SOW BABY SALAD leaves, Japanese onions, spinach and endive now.

IT'S TIME TO harvest the herb garden and have a good tidy-up. Cut away woody, 'leggy' and past-their-best plants and replace with new ones.

HERBS ARE FLOWERING and forming seeds at this time of year, so rather than letting the seeds go to waste, you can harvest them. Once dried, they can be stored and used for cooking and pickling. Harvest the seed heads when they have turned brown. Snip off the seed head along with around

5 centimetres of stem. Be sure to handle the seed heads carefully as they are brittle and fragile. Place the seed heads in a paper bag and, holding the bag closed, give the bag a good shake to dislodge the seeds. Be sure to use a different bag for each type of seed. Leave the bag for a week or so in a warm, dark, dry place, to allow the seeds to dry. Then give the seeds an extra shake, by which time the seeds should be dry and come away easily from the seed heads. Open the bag and remove the stems and transfer the seeds to an airtight metal, glass or plastic container. Be sure to use the seeds for seasoning food within six months for freshness and flavour. Seeds to gather include caraway, coriander, dill, angelica, chervil, anise and fennel.

ANOTHER JOB TO do in the herb garden in early autumn is to take semi-ripe and softwood cuttings for propagating over winter. Cuttings are a cheap and easy way to reproduce herb plants for next year. Semi-ripe means that the base of the stem for cutting is firm and only a little flexible in comparison to the soft stems of softwood cuttings. Make cuttings of

approximately 10 centimetres of the current season's growth. Then remove the leaves from the bottom two-thirds of the cutting before planting into pots containing compost mixed with a small amount of horticultural grit. Keep the cuttings well watered and place in a cool, shady spot in the greenhouse or indoors.

COLLECT UP ANNUAL herbs such as coriander, mint, basil and chives before the cold weather gets to them. These herbs can be frozen in ice cube trays with a little water and are then ready to use as and when you need them.

SOW ROCKET AND parsley in pots so you can bring them undercover during the frosts – a cold conservatory is an ideal spot to bring them into. The plants will be ready to harvest within eight weeks and can remain outside once established. Angelica seeds can also be sown, but plant these directly into the garden as they don't

take kindly to having their roots disturbed.
Angelica is particularly hardy and doesn't require
frost protection.

DIVIDE UP LARGE clumps of herbs during this
season and perhaps swap a few plants
with green-fingered friends.
Now is the time to plan next
year's herb garden.

PRUNE BACK SUMMER-FRUITING
raspberry canes by trimming those that held
fruit down to ground level. Select about eight of
the strongest new canes from each plant and trim
away the rest.

DRAW A PLAN of your vegetable plot and make a
note of what you have growing there. This will
be useful when it comes to planning for next year,
particularly in terms of crop rotation.

KEEP STRAWBERRY BEDS in good shape by thinning them and removing runners so that the main plants remain strong and healthy, and stand a better chance of producing a bumper crop next year.

ALTHOUGH NOT A typical garden plant, sloes (blackthorns) growing in the wild are ready to be picked after the first autumn frost. Sloe gin is a popular way of utilising these astringent fruits. Here's a simple recipe:

Sloe Gin

Decant half a litre of gin into an empty bottle; you will only need half a litre of gin for this recipe. Prick or cut the sloes and place them into the bottle, enough so that the gin reaches the top. Add 150 grams of sugar and screw on the top. Then wait two months before drinking, but remember to agitate the bottle once a day.

SEPTEMBER IS THE best time to pick blackberries. To check if they're ready to harvest, pull the berry away from the stalk and core. If it does not come away easily, it isn't ripe. One of the tastiest things to make is a warming blackberry and apple crumble:

Blackberry and Apple Crumble

Sieve 340 grams of plain flour into a large bowl and mix with 120 grams of granulated sugar and 170 grams of unsalted butter to a crumble consistency. Sprinkle a little rum over six cooking apples (roughly chopped) and 250 grams of blackberries in an oven dish. Cover the fruit with the crumble mixture and sprinkle the top with brown sugar before cooking in a preheated oven at 180 degrees Celsius for 35–40 minutes until the crumble topping is golden brown. Test the apples with a knife to see that they have cooked all the way through.

SPEND A BIT of time in the greenhouse. Check for plants that have become pot-bound and require repotting. Wash down as many surfaces as you can in the greenhouse, as once pests and diseases take hold, they can spread at an alarming rate. Look out for whitefly. If there are a small number of them, simply squash them between your thumb and finger, but if there is an infestation, the introduction of a parasitic wasp is one of the most effective ways of eradicating them. These can be purchased from horticultural pest control companies.

PICK UP SOME vegetable plants from your local nursery for overwintering. There should be plenty of available space in the vegetable patch now that the summer crops have finished. Remember to clear the vegetable garden as far as possible first and to fork it over, adding a mulch or fresh compost to replace the nutrients displaced by the previous crops. Give the soil an extra boost by planting potassium-rich banana skins cut into

pieces. Keeping your vegetable patch packed with
crops over the winter will not only ensure lots of
fresh produce for the long chilly months ahead,
but it will also give you a good reason to get
outside in the fresh air. Sow onion sets, cabbages,
garlic, asparagus, broad beans, peas and pea
shoots.

To SPEED UP germination of pea shoots, before
planting out sprinkle some seeds on a piece of
damp kitchen towel on a plate for a few days. As
soon as the roots begin to develop, they can be
planted out quite closely together, around
3 centimetres apart. Plant in three lines
at 30 centimetres apart. As soon as
the pea shoots appear, you can
pick these off and add them to
salads and stir-fries. They have
a lovely fresh, sweet flavour.

SOME VARIETIES OF onion sets can be planted
out now and will be ready for harvesting early
next year. Check the instructions on the seed
packet for information.

SOW HARDY VARIETIES of winter lettuce along with lamb's lettuce now, but give the seeds a bit of protection from the chilly weather by covering them in horticultural fleece or polythene. You should be rewarded with fresh lettuce for the salad bowl throughout the winter.

NOW THAT THE weather is getting cooler, it's time to bring the citrus plants indoors. They can scorch in a warm, dry atmosphere, so keep them away from centrally heated areas – a cool conservatory is best.

FIG TREES WILL need to be protected from frost, so cover them with horticultural fleece or netting filled with straw for insulation. This will ensure that any embryonic figs survive and continue to grow next year.

GIVE YOUR BRUSSELS sprout plants a bit of a boost with some mulch. Draw the mulch up around the stems to help firm up the plants and add some supporting canes to any particularly tall stems.

TEST GRAPES TO see if they are ripe for picking. They should be sweet and full of flavour. Once the grapes have changed colour it can take up to three weeks before they are ready for harvesting, so keep testing them every few days for sweetness. Another indicator of ready-to-pick grapes is the colour of the seeds, which will be brown rather than green. Once they are ready for harvesting, try not to touch the grapes when picking them, but instead hold the stalk above the bunch and sever the stalk where it joins the lateral vine – secateurs can help with this job. Grapes will not ripen further after picking and are best enjoyed straight from the vine.

Notes

....
....
....
....
....
....
....
....
....
....
....
....
....
....
....
....
....
....

Early Autumn

....
....
....
....
....
....
....
....
....
....
....
....
....
....
....
....
....
....
....

Late Autumn

PLANT GARLIC IN soil mixed with well-rotted manure, allowing 15 centimetres between cloves and 30 centimetres between rows. Garlic is a difficult plant to propagate and you should always grow it from a plant rather than from part of a bulb purchased from the supermarket, because shop-bought garlic can carry disease. Gently bruise the garlic cloves between your thumb and forefinger before planting, as this will make them more flavoursome. Keep in a cold frame, watering fortnightly before replanting outside in the spring. When the plants are established, it is important that you remove the flower buds so all the plant's energy is concentrated on forming the bulb.

PURCHASE SOME ONE-YEAR-OLD rhubarb plants from a garden centre and plant them out as soon as you can to ensure a harvest next year. Keep in mind that many varieties of rhubarb can grow

into very large plants and require plenty of space.
Place the top of the plant on or just below the
surface. Firm the surrounding soil and water well.

ONCE THE ARTICHOKE harvest has finished,
cut back the stems and insulate the crowns for
overwintering by covering them with a thick layer
of straw or chippings.

PRUNE AND TAKE cuttings of hardwood plants,
such as currants, figs, grapes and gooseberries.
Make sure sunlight can reach the stems and the
bushes are thinned out enough so that the air
can circulate, as this helps them to fruit well
and reduces the risk of disease.

HAVE A NOVEMBER bonfire and burn
any dead or diseased plants that
are unfit for composting.

PICK THE REMAINING tomatoes and ripen any green
ones by placing them in a paper bag or Kilner jar

with a ripe banana in a warm place, but away from
direct sunlight. The ethylene gas that the banana
gives off will ripen the tomatoes within one to two
weeks. Check regularly, and if your banana shows
signs of rot, simply replace it with a new one.

CLEAR AWAY AND compost greenhouse
plants, such as tomato, aubergine
and pepper, once the crops have
finished. Look out for blight
or mould and dispose of
infected plants separately.

COLLECT UP ALL of your canes, stakes and nets
and give them a good clean before storing them in
a dry, sanitary environment.

WHEN THE FRUIT harvest has finished, treat the
trees and bushes to some mulch around the bases
to restore nutrients and reduce weed growth.

Composting

Now is a good time to begin a compost heap.
To create your own compost, first you will need
an appropriate container for the job. There are
countless designs to choose from; take a look in
local garden centres, on the Internet, or make
enquires with your local council. Once you have
your bin, to ensure the compost material breaks
down efficiently place it in a sunny/semi-shaded
spot to maximise available heat, and on soil
for good drainage and easy access to beneficial
bacteria, insects and worms.

Your compost pile should be no smaller than one
cubic metre. At this size the pile will generate
enough heat to decompose while still allowing
for sufficient airflow. Invest in a compost
thermometer from your local garden centre, and
remember that the ideal temperature for effective
composting is between 50 and 70 degrees Celsius.
This heat is achieved when enzymes break down
the molecules of the composting material.

Have a layer of twigs and branches at the
bottom of the heap to provide vertical airflow

through the material; on top of this mix in your browns and greens with thin layers of grass mowings, dead flowers, manure and straw. Sheep manure is probably the richest source of nutrients, just ahead of horse manure. Chances are, you can probably find both for free if you know a farmer or horse owner.

Don't add the following items to your compost pile: charcoal or coal ashes, which contain high amounts of sulphur; cat or dog droppings, which might contain disease; or weeds, which will only return disease back to the soil once you spread your compost. And unless you fancy attracting rats to your garden, avoid adding eggs or meat to the mix.

To give your compost a kick-start, throw a few shovelfuls of old manure, alfalfa or blood meal over it, and then add some more during the process as an extra boost. This will provide the compost with plenty of bacteria, giving the microbes energy to break down material.

Weed-free and pesticide-free grass clippings bring nitrogen to your compost – be sure to mix them in well to avoid smells, prevent a slimy texture and get the maximum benefit from the grass.

If you want your compost heap to remain active during winter, be sure to keep your bin in a place that gets lots of sunlight. Alternatively, insulate the sides with hay to keep the compost warm.

Turn your compost pile every two weeks for fast results. The finished compost should look and smell like rich, dark soil. Compost can be made in six to eight weeks, or it can take a year or more. The more effort you put in, the quicker you get compost.

Your compost pile should be moist all the way through so be sure to wet each new layer every time you add one.

Do not leave a finished compost pile standing unprotected as it will lose nutrients. Special breathable compost cover sheets can be found at any garden centre.

SOW SOME BASIL seed in pots and place on a windowsill, as this particular herb isn't hardy enough to overwinter. Parsley and mint will also benefit from being brought indoors at this time of year. Dig up decent clumps of them from your established plants and pot them on into containers with fresh compost and good drainage.

PROTECT OVERWINTERING HERBS with horticultural fleece or transplant them to a sheltered spot. Those in pots need to be raised off the ground, onto bricks or pot feet to prevent waterlogging and to keep drainage holes open.

POTS CONTAINING ANNUALS must be emptied once the harvest has finished. The soil can be composted and the pots cleaned and stored ready for use next year.

COLLECT UP LEAVES surrounding peach and nectarine trees that have suffered from leaf curl and burn or bin them, keeping them well away from your healthy plants and compost heap. This harmful fungus can severely deplete the leaves and fruit and in some cases destroy the tree. There are a number of methods that gardeners use to

prevent leaf curl, such as hanging mothballs from the branches, while others spray the trees twice a year, once in autumn and once in spring, with a copper-based spray.

PICK UP SOME bare-rooted fruit trees and bushes for planting from the garden centre. Keep the roots bagged and covered until ready to plant, as once the roots are dry the plant will die. Make sure that the root collar is just above the soil after planting. The root collar is the bulge just above the roots. It's important not to plant the tree any deeper than this as tree bark can begin to rot quickly when it comes into contact with soil. Keep pulling up weeds that appear around the tree and water regularly.

PLACE GREASE BANDS (available online and from garden centres) on the trunks of fruit trees and on stakes to protect them from species of moth with wingless females, which climb the trees to mate. The caterpillar offspring of these moths will devour the foliage and fruits. Place the grease band around half a metre above ground level.

IF YOU HAVE had a good harvest of pumpkins, and have plenty of leftover flesh after hollowing them out to make Halloween lanterns, why not make pumpkin pie? Here is a recipe for you to try:

Pumpkin Pie

First remove the seeds, which can be planted at a later date (see page 37), then cut the flesh into chunks. You will need approximately half a kilo of pumpkin flesh to fill a 30-centimetre tart tin. Steam the flesh to soften it, then drain and leave to cool. Meanwhile make a basic pastry to line the base of the tin, leaving an overhang. Bake blind until it is golden brown. Make the filling by blending together the softened pumpkin flesh with two eggs, 175 grams of sugar, 140 millilitres of double cream, a teaspoon each of cinnamon, allspice and ginger, and a little grated nutmeg until the mixture has a smooth consistency. Spoon the mixture into the pastry case and bake for an hour at 180 degrees Celsius. Serve warm with whipped cream.

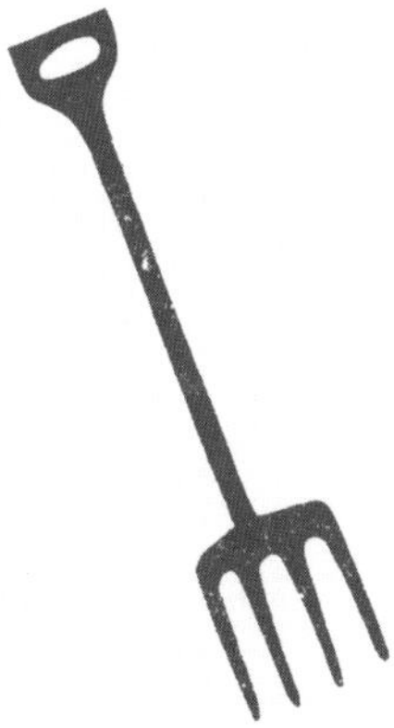

Notes

....

....

....

....

....

....

....

....

....

....

....

....

....

....

....

....

....

Late Autumn

....

....

....

....

....

....

....

....

....

....

....

....

....

....

....

....

....

....

Dried Fruit

Making dried fruit from your excess harvest will mean that you can enjoy your fruit crops for many months to come. Chop a variety of fruits into bite-size pieces. Dip the pieces into lemon juice before you begin the drying process, so they don't turn brown. Skewer whole grapes and cherries as this will ventilate the skins. Evenly space the fruit on a baking tray, and place in a cool oven at about 50 degrees Celsius. It will take several hours for the pieces to dry out completely. Once they have a nice, chewy texture, they are ready to eat. Keep them in an airtight container and eat within twelve months.

IF YOUR APPLE trees have suffered from apple scab this year (see page 32), you will need to rake up all of the fallen leaves and bin or burn them. This

is a fungal disease that can spread easily as the spores can scatter in wind or rain, so it may be the case that a neighbour's apple trees will also have suffered. If this has happened, ask them nicely to rake and destroy the leaves from their apple trees too, to reduce the risk of further infection.

START FEEDING CITRUS plants with a winter feed now. If you haven't done so already, bring your potted citrus plants indoors. Keep them in a cool room rather than one that is heated so that they don't dry out or scorch. When watering at this time of year, allow the surface of the soil to become touch-dry before watering. Overwatering is the commonest cause of stress in citrus plants, especially in winter.

HAVE A CAREFUL look at apple and pear trees for canker in the winter months, as it's much easier to spot when the branches have shed their leaves. Canker is a disease caused by a fungus. The cankers are sunken into the bark and are round or oval in appearance. They appear at a bud or wound (i.e. where the bark is broken) and can be pruned away. Make sure that these infected branches and spurs are binned or burned.

BENEFIT NEXT YEAR'S crop of runner beans, squashes and pumpkins by digging a compost trench. Make a hole or trench a spade deep and wide and fill it with kitchen scraps as and when they become available. Cover each layer of kitchen scraps with soil or compost from your heap and repeat the process until the trench is full. Leave the trench until it's time to sow the crops. See pages 102–103 for information on what can and can't be composted.

TREAT YOUR VEG patch once you have harvested your autumn vegetables by digging out any weeds and going over the ground with a good dose of compost and manure, then spread old rugs or an unwanted carpet over the area for the winter to suffocate any weeds. You'll have the perfect base to start spring planting next year.

RHUBARB PLANTS NEED to be divided every five years or so, but only when dormant, i.e. during the winter. Split the plants with a spade into three or four crowns, making sure each crown has an eye to provide next year's shoots.

IF YOU HAVE established fig trees, now is the time to prune them, in the dormant season, when they are not growing. Select around six branches as 'fruiting wood' – the healthiest branches that will carry the fruit – and prune away the rest, especially those containing dead and diseased wood. Remove any suckers that have appeared at the base of the tree as well. The next stage of pruning is to remove any secondary branches that are growing at an angle of less than 45 degrees from the main branches. This is important because if left they could grow too close to the trunk and produce poor-quality fruit. The final stage is to cut back the main branches by a quarter so that the tree concentrates its energies on producing larger, sweeter fruit.

YOUR FRUIT PLANTS need protection over winter, not just from frost because birds can be a particular problem as they like to eat the buds at this time of year, which in turn significantly affects plant growth and crop yield. A fruit cage is one solution. Make your own with four canes or wooden posts, one on each corner of the plot, with an old upturned flowerpot capping each cane. Then lay netting over the top and weigh it down around the edges with bricks or large stones. Home-made fruit cages often last longer than the shop-bought ones and cost a fraction of the price.

PRUNE AUTUMN-FRUITING raspberries once winter has set in. Begin by cutting the old canes back to ground level. Tie new stems to supports as they grow, using pieces of fabric cut from an old pair of tights or a jersey garment – the fabric will stretch as the plants grow without damaging them. Take a look at your summer-fruiting raspberry plants too, because although you might have pruned them back in the autumn, new growth will have appeared by now and it's important to trim back the top growth so that the canes only protrude around 20 centimetres above the top of the support.

 *Early Winter*

NEW SUMMER-FRUITING raspberry canes can be
planted out during the winter, or dormant season,
from November right through until February.
Select a plot that receives plenty of sunshine and
is slightly sheltered. Raspberries can be purchased
as bare-root canes or in pots, but both must be
planted in winter. First check that the plot isn't
frozen or waterlogged, then make sure it is free
from weeds as it's difficult to weed round
raspberry canes once they have become
established. Plant them 50 centimetres
apart, then add an organic mulch round
the bases. Once planted, prune the
canes to within 25 centimetres of
the ground.

EARLY WINTER IS the main pruning period for
grapevines, although it is necessary to keep on
top of pruning and maintenance throughout the
growing season (see page 40). Prune back old
wood and trim away any new buds in order to
stimulate new crop growth.

Notes

....
....
....
....
....
....
....
....
....
....
....
....
....
....
....
....
....
....

Early Winter

....
....
....
....
....
....
....
....
....
....
....
....
....
....
....
....
....
....

Late Winter

EVEN IN THE depths of winter there are plenty of edible crops that can be planted, such as broad beans, Brassicas, carrots, cucumbers, garlic, onions and shallots, parsnips, leeks and horseradish.

BEGIN CHITTING POTATOES from late January to early February in the greenhouse or cold frame, or a cool room in the house. Stand the tubers blunt end up in trays. Make sure they receive plenty of daylight and wait until the shoots are roughly 2 centimetres long before planting out.

PLANT GARLIC AND onion seeds in the greenhouse or cool conservatory. They respond well to cooler temperatures, about 10 to 15 degrees Celsius. Sow five seeds of either garlic or onion into each pot containing damp compost. Cover with vermiculite. The bulbs (mini onions) should be ready to plant out in the spring (see page 21).

SHALLOTS ARE AVAILABLE from garden centres for planting out now. They have a lovely sweet and delicate flavour, and once harvested they can be stored successfully in the same way as onions – see page 63 for information on storing onions.

GIVE YOUR CITRUS plants some attention as they may require pruning now. Begin by trimming down any leggy branches by around two-thirds and removing overcrowded branches. Cut away any shoots that are growing out of the bottom or middle portions of the branches. These 'water shoots' can be fast-growing, so keep a regular lookout for these and prune them as they appear.

THE MOST IMPORTANT time to prune fruit trees is in late winter before you see any signs of new growth. Prune off damaged limbs as well as smaller branches that grow too close to the main branches. Use antibacterial wipes when cleaning your pruners between cuts to keep your plants healthy and disease-free. Only prune 'open grown' trees at this time of year, and not those trained against walls.

CONTINUE TO INSPECT your stored produce for rodent activity and damage. Remove and compost any fruit or vegetables that have been nibbled on or are showing signs of decay.

THERE IS STILL a bit of harvesting to be done in the depths of winter. Leeks will be ready to pull up now, as will parsnips, Brussels sprouts and winter cabbage, beans and peas, chard, celery, turnips, winter lettuce, cauliflower, kale, winter spinach and celeriac.

WARMING SOUP IS the perfect recipe for using up vegetables and keeping the cold away during the long, dark days of winter. Here's a simple recipe:

Vegetable Soup

Chop up a large onion and a garlic clove and
sautés in olive oil in a saucepan until soft.
Add a litre of cold water, four diced carrots
and two diced celery sticks, and simmer for
approximately half an hour. Add a can of
chopped tomatoes and a litre of chicken or
vegetable stock, and bring the mixture to the
boil before simmering for a further five minutes.
Remove from the heat and add some herbs, such
as basil and thyme, along with salt and pepper
to taste. Serve with warm crusty bread.

IF YOU HAVEN'T already done so, it's a good
time to start digging beds for next season. Dig
up and compost any remaining vegetation, but
be careful not to compost any diseased plants –
these must be binned or burned. Cover the soil
with black polythene or old carpets to stifle any
weed growth.

Late Winter

IF YOU HAVEN'T already done so, protect any newly sown crops from birds by constructing a cage (see page 114 for information on how to make one).

ENJOY SOME TIME indoors and peruse seed catalogues as you plan which goodies you will be growing next year in your edible garden. Order seed potatoes and onion sets now.

FRUIT TREES AND bushes will need protection from frost damage at this time of year. Those that blossom early, such as peach, are particularly vulnerable, so cover with horticultural fleece at night but remove it during the day to allow the air to circulate and pollinators to do their job. Fruit plants that have been trained against fences or walls will also need a covering of fleece or netting at night. Use bamboo canes so that the netting does not touch the fragile blossom.

CLEAN OUT THE greenhouse inside and out and insulate with bubble wrap. Clear the guttering of leaves and debris. Check over the heater, refuelling if necessary, and make sure it's working effectively.

IF YOU FANCY some early salad vegetables, you could try the Victorian art of hotbedding. A hotbed is a warm environment for producing early vegetables using heat generated from decomposing organic matter. Make a wooden frame the size that you want your hotbed in the same way that you would make a raised bed (see page 124). Find a sunny spot in the garden and dig a hole 3 feet deep. Place a layer of straw at the bottom of the hole about a foot deep and then fill the rest of the hole with hot, fresh manure (about four to six weeks old). Cow and chicken manure is best for hotbeds. Put a 10-centimetre layer of straw on top of the manure and then place regular garden soil on top. Sow salad seeds in the normal way and water them. Place the wooden frame over the hotbed to help keep the heat in. If it's particularly cold, place a piece of glass or clear plastic over it, as this will allow the sunlight through to the seedlings but protect them from frost. The hotbed will give your vegetables a jump-start and maximise the growing season.

TAKE A LOOK at your grapevines now for signs of infestation. Use a sharp knife and remove any loose pieces of bark to expose any destructive pests that might be hiding there. Pesticides should be avoided when dealing with infestations, instead release predatory insects, such as ladybirds and parasitic wasps, to feed on the pests.

PLANT BARE-ROOTED walnut trees now. Purchase a bare-root at around a metre tall. See page 105 for information on planting bare-rooted trees.

IF YOU'RE GOING to build raised beds, now is a good time to do it while things are quieter in the garden. Raised beds are surprisingly simple and cheap to make. First you need to decide where it should be situated and peg out a perfect rectangle or square using canes or tent pegs and string. The widest part of the raised bed area shouldn't be greater than 1.5 metres to allow for easy access to the centre of the bed without having to physically get in it. You will need four planks of wood, or

deck boards, and between four and eight hinge brackets and enough screws to fit them with. The wood will need to be treated to safeguard against rot. Remove the string but keep the canes in place and dig out the raised bed, at least a spade's depth. Assemble the wooden frame by joining each corner with one or two metal brackets – depending on the height of the frame. It's best to assemble on site as the finished frames are very heavy and would require several people to lift into place. Fill the raised bed with fresh compost, which must then be compacted down by treading on it. The compost in the middle of the bed must be slightly higher than the frame to allow for settling. Use a handful of sharpened wooden pegs to secure the bed in place and give the frame a bit of extra support, then plant out your seeds or seedlings in the normal way. If making early plantings, place a piece of plastic or glass over the frame at night for frost protection.

CHECK TO SEE if any trees are shading your vegetable plot and prune them back where necessary.

Notes

....
....
....
....
....
....
....
....
....
....
....
....
....
....
....
....
....